Cambridge **Discovery Education**™

▶ **INTERACTIVE READERS**

Series editor: Bob Hastings

TRAFFIC JAMS

THE ROAD AHEAD

A1

Simon Beaver

CAMBRIDGE
UNIVERSITY PRESS

Discovery
EDUCATION™

CAMBRIDGE UNIVERSITY PRESS
Cambridge, New York, Melbourne, Madrid, Cape Town,
Singapore, São Paulo, Delhi, Mexico City

Cambridge University Press
32 Avenue of the Americas, New York, NY 10013-2473, USA

www.cambridge.org
Information on this title: www.cambridge.org/9781107674684

First published 2014
Reprinted 2014

Printed in Hong Kong, China, by Golden Cup Printing Company Limited

A catalog record for this publication is available from the British Library.

Library of Congress Cataloging-in-Publication Data

Beaver, Simon.
  Traffic jams : the road ahead / Simon Beaver.
    pages cm. -- (Cambridge discovery interactive readers)
  ISBN 978-1-107-67468-4 (pbk. : alk. paper)
  1. Traffic congestion--Juvenile literature. 2. English language--Textbooks for foreign speakers.
3. Readers (Elementary) I. Title.

HE336.C64B43 2013
388.3'14--dc23

                            2013023921

ISBN 978-1-107-67468-4

Additional resources for this publication at www.cambridge.org

Layout services, art direction, book design, and photo research: Q2ABillSMITH GROUP
Editorial services: Hyphen S.A.
Audio production: CityVox, New York
Video production: Q2ABillSMITH GROUP

Contents

Before You Read:
Get Ready!

There are now more than 1,000,000,000 (one billion) vehicles in the world! What can we do about traffic?

Words to Know

Look at the pictures. Complete the sentences below with the correct words.

vehicles

traffic

traffic jam

police

park/parking space

lane

❶ You're driving too fast! Do you want the _____ to stop you?

❷ I'm sorry I'm late. I was in a _____ .

❸ You can _____ your car here. Look! There's a _____ .

❹ That _____ is only for buses.

❺ I like to drive at night when there isn't much _____ .

❻ There were a lot of _____ on the road.

Words to Know

Read the paragraph. Use the highlighted words to complete the sentences below.

I like to cycle to work. It's only a kilometer. But today, I was on a little street in the city center, and a car parked in front of me. It was impossible to cycle around the car. The driver had green hair. He looked very strange! I asked him to move the car, but he said no.

1. That's _____! I can't find my key.
2. I walked _____ the house to get to the back door.
3. I didn't _____ here, I took the bus.
4. There are a lot of stores in the _____.
5. Did you _____ my glasses? I can't find them.

Comparatives

Look at the cars. Then, read the sentences below and write T (True) or F (False).

Bob's car	Mahmoud's car	Ji-min's car
$500	$20,000	$50,000

1. _____ Mahmoud's car is <u>more</u> expensive <u>than</u> Bob's car.
2. _____ Ji-min's car is <u>less</u> expensive <u>than</u> Bob's car.
3. _____ Ji-min's car is <u>the most</u> expensive.
4. _____ Mahmoud's car is <u>the cheapest</u>.
5. _____ Mahmoud's car is probably <u>easier</u> to drive than Ji Min's car.
6. _____ Bob's car is <u>safer</u> than Mahmoud's car.
7. _____ Ji-min's car is <u>the fastest</u>.

CHAPTER 1

Traffic

LIFE IS FAST IN BUSY CITIES, BUT TRAFFIC IS SLOW. WHAT'S THE ANSWER?

Today, we have a big problem: **traffic**! There are too many cars in cities and sometimes outside cities, too.

This isn't a new problem. Before cars, people used **vehicles** with horses. There were a lot of them, and they made a lot of noise! A famous English writer, Samuel Pepys, wrote about London traffic jams 350 years ago!

Today, people often don't live near their work. In many places, there aren't many trains and buses, and they're expensive. So people drive to work.

A lot of people use their cars to go into cities in the morning and home in the evening. Often, there's only one person in each car. And there are too many cars. In Tokyo, New York, London, and other big cities the traffic goes very slowly, only 15 **kilometers** an hour! Bicycles travel faster!

It can be hard to **park**, too. Sometimes, almost half the cars in a city center are looking for a place to park. In some cities, there is only one parking space for every two cars!

Video Quest

Traffic Dreams

Watch the video. Why do the people want to make a new kind of car?

Traffic lanes

CHAPTER 2

Finding Answers

TRAFFIC IS A PROBLEM, BUT WHAT CAN DRIVERS DO ABOUT IT?

In places where traffic is bad, drivers find different answers to the problem.

People who live in the same place can have a carpool – they go to work and come home in the same car. They often use a different person's car each day. There's less traffic when three or four people use only one car.

In some countries there are **special** fast lanes for carpools. Cars with only one person can't use these lanes.

Many drivers have no other person in their car. But they want to use the fast lanes. So some of them put a big doll in their car! They want the police to think the doll is a person. But if the police stop the driver, he or she has to pay a fine.[1]

People say some funny things when police stop them in a fast lane. One time, the police stopped a woman. She was the only person in the car. But she said, "It's OK. I'm going to have a baby! I'm two people!" She had to pay the fine.

[1] **fine:** money you must pay when you do something wrong

? UNDERSTAND
What is a carpool?

To use fast lanes, people also use "casual carpooling." Some people wait in a place near a road with a fast lane. Drivers see that people are waiting there. They stop and give them a ride. They don't know the people. But they want another person in their car. Then they can use the fast lane.

Why don't more people take **public transportation** to go to work? In many cities, buses and trains are fast and not expensive. The problem is that many people really like their cars.

GPS

GPS tells you how to get to your destination.[2] But does GPS help drivers to go faster? And does it stop traffic jams?

Maybe. It's easier for drivers with GPS to get to their destination. They don't have to drive for a long time to find the right street. So there's less traffic. And some kinds of GPS show where the traffic isn't moving. Drivers can take a different road and stay out of traffic jams.

[2] **destination:** the place you're going to

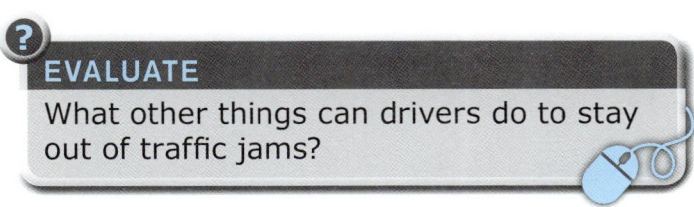
❓ EVALUATE
What other things can drivers do to stay out of traffic jams?

CHAPTER 3

No Parking!

IN THE CITY, YOU CAN'T PARK! WHAT'S THE ANSWER?

Drivers are unhappy when they can't find a parking space. In big cities, sometimes 40 percent of cars are looking for a space. In Freiburg, Germany, at one time it was 74 percent of cars! All those vehicles **move** slowly around the streets. They make traffic jams.

Drivers don't like to pay to park. But if they don't have to pay, more people use their cars. So there are too many cars for the number of parking spaces. What are the answers to this problem?

One answer is a congestion charge – money that you pay to drive in a city. Drivers in London have to pay £10 ($16) a day. Cameras take photos of the license plates on cars. Computers check if the drivers paid the congestion charge. If not, they have to pay a fine.

A license plate

Another answer is good, cheap public transportation: buses, trains, and trams. Paris now has 15 percent less parking than ten years ago. But it has more bus lanes. Buses travel faster. More people park their cars outside Paris and take the train or bus into the city now.

A tram

ANALYZE
Why are buses faster in Paris now?

Elephants

When drivers park in the wrong place, they have to pay a fine. How much money do cities get from these fines? With 22,000 fines each day, New York City makes $600 **million** a year! But Sydney, Australia, only made $13 million last year. More drivers park in the right place in Sydney.

Vehicles get fines, but what about animals? There's an old law[3] in Florida. It says that if you leave an elephant in a parking space, you have to pay. If not, you get a fine!

[3]**law:** laws say what people must or must not do in a country

A lot of people want to drive into cities. And when it's cheap to park in a city center, there are too many cars, and it isn't possible to find a parking space.

That's why it can be very expensive to park in some cities – $89 a day in Oslo, Norway. In London, you can pay about $1,000 a month for a city center parking space. But maybe the most expensive parking space in the world was in Greenwich Village in New York City in 2012. To buy it you needed $1,000,000!

Video Quest

Sideways

Watch the video about making a new car. What is the problem with the new wheels?

An alien

CHAPTER 4

Strange Travelers

THINK ABOUT HOW WE TRAVEL. STRANGE, ISN'T IT?

In Ben Elton's book *Gridlock,* aliens come to our world to learn about people. They look at the places where we live and work, and how we travel. But they don't understand cars. They see that every morning hundreds of millions of people get into big boxes. These boxes take the people many kilometers to their workplace. But often, the big boxes can't move because there are so many of them. Then, in the evening, the people get into their boxes and slowly drive home again.

The aliens think this is really **strange**. Why don't people travel in the faster boxes they call trains and buses? Or live near their workplace? Do they like to sit in boxes for hours? Or aren't they very smart?

The aliens are right. Why don't we live near our workplaces?

It's often because houses are too expensive in the city. People who lived in the city before have to live outside it now. But many jobs are in the city center. Cheaper houses in cities are a possible answer to traffic problems.

For a lot of our lives, we sit in traffic jams. But that's not the only problem with traffic. Smoke from our cars is bad for trees, plants – and us! And it's making the world hotter. That may be our biggest problem in a few years.

Bicycles are a good answer. They don't make smoke. They're good for our bodies and they're fun. But cycling to work can be hard. Very hard if you live many kilometers from your workplace.

Working at home is also good for traffic – and people. With computers and the Internet, many people work at home now.

? EVALUATE

What can you do to help on the next World Carfree Day?

Do you know about World Carfree Day? On September 22, all around the world, people leave their cars at home. They take the bus or train, or they cycle to work. Some people walk if they live near their workplace.

Why is World Carfree Day a good thing? First, because for one day a year there's less traffic. But also because it helps people to think about the problem of traffic. They see that buses and trains aren't so bad. Or that cycling and walking are good for them.

A smart parking meter in Copenhagen

CHAPTER 5

What Do You Think?

DO YOU LIVE OR WORK IN A CITY? WHICH CHANGE DO YOU WANT?

Here are three possible answers to traffic problems. What do you think about them?

1. In some cities like San Francisco and Copenhagen, there is a new answer to help drivers find parking spaces. There is now a computer "eye" in each space. It sees if a car is there. Drivers can use their smartphone to see which spaces they can use. And the police computer can see which cars stay too long in a space. The drivers of those cars have to pay a fine.

Traffic lights   Street signs

2. In some cities, people can't drive cars in certain places. They must walk, cycle, or use public transportation. But it can be expensive for a city to make bicycle lanes and pay for good public transportation.

3. On streets in Drachten, in the Netherlands, there are no traffic lights or road signs. Drivers must drive slowly and watch for people and other vehicles. Some people think this makes the streets less safe, but it really makes the streets a lot safer. Other towns in Europe are doing the same thing.

Which of these ideas do you want to see in your city or town? Why?

Video Quest

Park It!

Watch the video to see if the new vehicle works. What does the policeman think?

After You Read

Choose Ⓐ (True) or Ⓑ (False). If the book does not tell you, choose Ⓒ (Doesn't say).

❶ There were traffic jams in London 350 years ago.

- Ⓐ True
- Ⓑ False
- Ⓒ Doesn't say

❷ There are more carpools in Sweden than in Denmark.

- Ⓐ True
- Ⓑ False
- Ⓒ Doesn't say

❸ GPS can show traffic jams.

- Ⓐ True
- Ⓑ False
- Ⓒ Doesn't say

❹ A congestion charge is money you pay to park.

- Ⓐ True
- Ⓑ False
- Ⓒ Doesn't say

❺ You never pay more than $50 a day to park in Oslo.

- Ⓐ True
- Ⓑ False
- Ⓒ Doesn't say

❻ Smoke from cars is bad for fish.

- Ⓐ True
- Ⓑ False
- Ⓒ Doesn't say

7 San Francisco uses computer "eyes" in parking spaces.

(A) True

(B) False

(C) Doesn't say

8 In Drachten, the streets are not safe because there are no road signs.

(A) True

(B) False

(C) Doesn't say

What's the Answer?

Write down three traffic problems in your country. What do people do about these problems? Do these answers work? Why or why not?

Problems in my country	Answers	Do they work? Why or why not?
1.		
2.		
3.		

Choose the Correct Words

Complete the paragraph with the correct words from the box.

lanes	public transportation	traffic	traffic jam

Together, the vehicles on a road are called **1** _____.
Vehicles can't move when they're in a **2** _____.
Buses, trains, and trams are called **3** _____. In
many cities, buses can drive in special **4** _____.

Answer Key

Words to Know, page 4
1 police **2** traffic jam **3** park/parking space **4** lane
5 traffic **6** vehicles

Words to Know, page 5
1 strange **2** around **3** cycle **4** city center **5** move

Comparatives, page 5
1 T **2** F **3** T **4** F **5** T **6** F **7** T

Video Quest, page 7 *Answers will vary.*

Understand, page 9
People who go to work in the same car each day have
a carpool.

Evaluate, page 11 *Answers will vary.*

Analyze, page 13
Because there are more bus lanes and less parking for cars.

Video Quest, page 15
They only work if the vehicle moves slowly.

Evaluate, page 19 *Answers will vary.*

Video Quest, page 21
The policeman doesn't know if they parked the vehicle
right. He never saw anything like this before.

True or False?, page 22
1 A **2** C **3** A **4** B **5** B **6** C **7** A **8** B

What's the Answer?, page 23 *Answers will vary.*

Choose the Correct Words, page 23
1 traffic **2** traffic jam **3** public transportation **4** lanes